SHARING STORIES
MAKING MEMORIES

SHARING STORIES
Making Memories ✳

A Journal for Grandparents and Grandchildren

BY

SCARLET PAOLICCHI

ILLUSTRATIONS BY IRENA FREITAS

ROCKRIDGE PRESS

Interior and Cover Designer: Peatra Jariya
Editor: Ada Fung
Production Manager: Oriana Siska
Production Editor: Melissa Edeburn
Art Producer: Sue "Bees" Bischofberger
Illustration © Irena Freitas/Illozoo, 2019

ISBN: Print 978-1-64152-636-4

CONTENTS

INTRODUCTION

The opportunity to connect across generations is a special one. The bond between a grand-parent and a grandchild can be such a source of joy, love, and guidance. It can also be something more—a passing of the torch, a chance to share family lore and family values while learning about the new stars in the family line.

My grandparents had a profound influence on me, and though they are gone now, I feel so fortunate to have gotten to know them as well as I did. My paternal grandparents were amazing role models for me, and my maternal grandmother and I shared a special bond. I have so many happy memories of us gardening and cooking together, and just sitting around and chatting. She had a home office, and I would hang out with her there, cutting and taping things up and playing pretend office while she worked. She'd call me "Scarlet Scissors" because she was always finding bits of scrap paper I had left under her desk. All through my childhood, she was my go-to source for solid advice and selfless love, and I miss her and all my other grandparents dearly.

My kids are also lucky to have close relationships with their grandparents—each special and unique in its own way. Whether they're having family jam sessions on the piano and clarinet with Grandma or playing card games and debating sports with Grandpa, my children find that their grandparents are a great source of information and entertainment.

We all lead such busy lives, and we're often separated from family by geography, which can make it challenging to develop true bonds. This journal is meant to help grandparents and grandchildren engage with each other, connect with each other on a deeper level, and see each other as more than *just* the grandparent or the grandchild. I hope that writing in this journal will allow my own kids to learn more about their grandparents (and that, yes, they were young once, too!) and that it will allow my parents to gain more insight into their grandkids' lives and their hopes and dreams for the future.

This is your chance to get all your questions answered—including ones you may not have even thought to ask! Grandkids, this is your chance to find out all about what your grandparents were like when they were your age—where they lived, what their favorite hobbies were, and what their lives were like. Grandparents, this is your chance to learn all about what makes your grandkids tick—what makes them laugh, what they like to do, and who their role models are. With this journal, you're not just preserving memories—you're making them.

The journal is organized by theme and laid out with facing pages that have similar questions for the grandchild and the grandparent to answer; the pages for each are labeled Grandchild or Grandparent. At the end of each chapter, there are blank Q&A pages so you can write in your own questions. Feel free to go in order or skip around to the sections that interest you most.

There are many ways to fill out this journal. You can sit down together in person or use a phone call or video chat to share answers. You can swap the journal back and forth if you see each other fairly regularly. You can even stick it in the mail! There is no wrong way to use it. No matter how you complete the journal, you'll be making memories together that you will cherish forever.

CHAPTER 1

All About Us

Grandchild

My full name is ....

You call me ....

What is the story behind your name? Were you named after someone? Why did your parents choose this name?

....

....

....

....

....

Do you have any nicknames?

....

....

....

GRANDPARENT

My full name is ....

You call me ....

What is the story behind your name? Were you named after someone? Why did your parents choose this name?

....

....

....

....

....

Do you (or did you) have any nicknames?

....

....

....

Grandchild

My date of birth is ....

I am .... years old.

I was born in ....

Are there any special or funny stories surrounding your birth?

....

....

....

....

What has been your favorite age so far, and why?

....

....

....

....

GRANDPARENT

My date of birth is ....

I am .... years old.

I was born in ....

Are there any special or funny stories surrounding your birth?

....

....

....

....

What has been your favorite age so far, and why?

....

....

....

....

Grandchild

I currently live in .... , and I have lived here for .... years.

How and why did your family choose the place where you live?

....

....

....

Where else have you lived? List all the places you have called home and a special thing about each one, including where you live now.

....

....

....

....

....

GRANDPARENT

I currently live in ...., and I have lived here for .... years.

How and why did you choose the place where you live?

....

....

....

Where else have you lived? List all the places you have called home and a special thing about each one, including where you live now.

....

....

....

....

....

....

OUR FAMILY

GREAT GRANDPARENTS

....

GRANDPARENT

....

....

GREAT GRANDPARENTS

....

GRANDPARENT

....

....

GREAT GRANDPARENTS

....

GRANDPARENT

....

....

GREAT GRANDPARENTS

....

GRANDPARENT

....

GRANDCHILD

....

SIBLING

....

PARENT

....

SIBLING

....

PARENT

....

SIBLING

....

Grandchild

PASTE IN OR DRAW A PHOTO OF US TOGETHER TODAY.

GRANDPARENT

PASTE IN OR DRAW A PHOTO OF THE DAY WE MET FOR THE FIRST TIME.

Q:

A:

Q:

A:

13

CHAPTER 2

My Favorite Things

Grandchild

My favorite color is ....

My favorite thing to do is ....

What makes you laugh?

....

....

....

....

What is your favorite possession? Where did you get it, or who gave it to you?

....

....

....

....

....

GRANDPARENT

My favorite color is ....

My favorite thing to do is ....

What makes you laugh?

....

....

....

....

What is your favorite possession? Where did you get it, or who gave it to you?

....

....

....

....

....

Grandchild

Some of my favorite musical artists or groups are ....

....

....

When do you most enjoy listening to music?

....

....

What types of TV shows or movies do you like to watch?

....

....

List three of your favorite books:

....

....

....

GRANDPARENT

Some of my favorite musical artists or groups are ....

....

....

When do you most enjoy listening to music?

....

....

What types of TV shows or movies do you like to watch?

....

....

List three of your favorite books:

....

....

....

Grandchild

My favorite hobby is ....

How did you pick it up, and why is it your favorite?

....

....

....

List a few of your favorite sports or outdoor activities and what you most enjoy about each:

....

....

....

....

....

....

GRANDPARENT

My favorite hobby is ....

How did you pick it up, and why is it your favorite?

....

....

....

List a few of your favorite sports or outdoor activities and what you most enjoy about each:

....

....

....

....

....

....

Grandchild

My favorite breakfast is ....

....

My favorite dinner is ....

....

My favorite dessert is ....

....

Share a favorite food memory:

....

....

....

....

....

GRANDPARENT

My favorite breakfast is ....

....

My favorite dinner is ....

....

My favorite dessert is ....

....

Share a favorite food memory:

....

....

....

....

....

Q:

....

....

....

A:

....

....

....

....

....

....

....

Q:

A:

CHAPTER 3

Our Family and Traditions

Grandchild

What are your parents' names, and where were they born?

....

....

Do you have any siblings? If so, list them, and yourself, from oldest to youngest:

....

....

In what ways are you like your parents, and in what ways are you different?

....

....

....

What is it like having siblings? If you don't have any, what do you think it would be like if you did?

....

....

GRANDPARENT

What are your parents' names, and where were they born?

....

....

Do you have any siblings? If so, list them, and yourself, from oldest to youngest:

....

....

In what ways are you like your parents, and in what ways are you different?

....

....

....

What was it like growing up with siblings? If you didn't have any, what do you think it would have been like if you had?

....

....

Grandchild

My family's ethnicity is ....

What ethnic heritage traditions do you celebrate? If you don't celebrate any, which ones would you be interested in celebrating or learning more about?

....

....

....

....

Share your favorite family story that has been passed down:

....

....

....

....

GRANDPARENT

My family's ethnicity is ....

Did you celebrate any ethnic heritage traditions as a kid that you don't celebrate any-more? What were they?

....

....

....

....

....

Share a family story that I may not know:

....

....

....

....

Grandchild

If your family is religious, what are some of the ways you celebrate and practice your faith?

....

....

....

What are some important values to your family, and how do you put those values into practice?

....

....

....

What are some sayings that you learned from your parents?

....

....

....

GRANDPARENT

If your family is religious, what are some of the ways you celebrate and practice your faith?

....

....

....

What are some important values to your family, and how do you put those values into practice?

....

....

....

What are some sayings that you learned from your parents?

....

....

....

Grandchild

What pastimes or hobbies do you share with your parents and siblings?

....

....

Tell me about a unique or unusual family tradition (for example, a themed meal night, silly birthday celebration, or special service project).

....

....

....

What are some of your family's special recipes, and where did they come from? Do you help make them?

....

....

....

....

GRANDPARENT

What pastimes or hobbies do you share with your parents and siblings?

....

....

Tell me about a special tradition or routine that you had with your family when you were little.

....

....

....

What dish from your childhood do you miss? How is it made? (Include a recipe if you have one.)

....

....

....

....

Grandchild

What is your favorite family holiday tradition, and why?

....

....

....

If you could start another family holiday tradition, what would it be?

....

....

Tell a funny holiday story:

....

....

....

....

GRANDPARENT

What is your favorite family holiday tradition, and why?

....

....

....

If you could start another family holiday tradition, what would it be?

....

....

Tell a funny holiday story from your childhood:

....

....

....

....

....

Grandchild

To whom in your family do feel closest, and why?

....

....

....

....

Is there a family member who you would like me to meet? Tell a story about that person.

....

....

....

....

....

....

....

GRANDPARENT

To whom in your family do you feel closest, and why?

....

....

....

....

Is there a family member who you wish I could have met? Tell a story about that person.

....

....

....

....

....

....

Q:

....

....

....

A:

....

....

....

....

....

....

Q:

A:

CHAPTER 4

Childhood

Grandchild

What is your earliest memory? How old were you? Where were you, and who was with you?

....

....

....

....

....

Describe a really fun day you had when you were younger:

....

....

....

....

....

GRANDPARENT

What is your earliest memory? How old were you? Where were you, and who was with you?

....

....

....

....

....

Describe a really fun day from your childhood:

....

....

....

....

....

Grandchild

List the things you do on a typical day:

....

....

....

What types of things do you do in your free time in the evenings or on weekends?

....

....

What chores are you responsible for?

....

....

What is your least favorite chore, and why?

....

....

GRANDPARENT

List the things you did on a typical day during your childhood:

....

....

....

What types of things did you do in your free time in the evenings or on weekends?

....

....

What chores were you responsible for as a child?

....

....

What was your least favorite chore, and why?

....

....

Grandchild

List your three favorite games:

....

....

....

The game I am best at is ....

....

The game that makes me laugh the most is ...., because

....

....

Is there a special toy or possession that you can never be without?

....

....

....

GRANDPARENT

List your three favorite childhood games:

....

....

....

The game I was best at is ....

....

The game that made me laugh the most was ...., because

....

....

Was there a special toy or possession that you could never be without as a kid?

....

....

....

Grandchild

What is your favorite room in your house, and why?

....

....

What do you like about your bedroom, and what would you change?

....

....

....

What is your neighborhood like?

....

....

Where is your favorite spot to hang out in the neighborhood?

....

....

GRANDPARENT

What was your childhood home like?

....

....

Describe your childhood bedroom:

....

....

....

Describe the neighborhood you grew up in:

....

....

Where was your favorite spot to hang out in the neighborhood?

....

....

Q:

A:

Q:

A:

CHAPTER 5

School Days

Grandchild

What is a typical day of school like for you?

....

....

....

....

How do you get to school?

....

What do you like most about school? What do you not like about it?

....

....

....

....

GRANDPARENT

What was a typical day of school like for you?

....

....

....

....

How did you get to school?

....

What did you like most about school? What did you not like about it?

....

....

....

....

....

Grandchild

My favorite school subject is .... ,

because ....

....

My least favorite school subject is .... ,

because ....

....

My favorite teacher ever is .... ,

because ....

....

My least favorite teacher ever is .... ,

because ....

....

GRANDPARENT

My favorite school subject was .... ,

because ....

....

My least favorite school subject was .... ,

because ....

....

My favorite teacher ever was .... ,

because ....

....

My least favorite teacher ever was .... ,

because ....

....

Grandchild

What fun elective classes do you take at school or outside school? Why do you enjoy them?

....

....

What musical instrument do you play, and do you enjoy it? If you don't play an instrument, which one would you most like to try?

....

....

Do you study a second language? If so, which one? If not, which language would you most like to learn?

....

....

If you could take any class you wanted, what would it be?

....

....

GRANDPARENT

Did you take any elective classes at school or outside school? What were they, and why did you enjoy them?

....

....

Did you learn a musical instrument when you were a kid, and did you enjoy it? If you didn't play an instrument, is there one you'd like to pick up now?

....

....

Did you study a second language? If so, which one? If you didn't, what language would you most like to learn now?

....

....

If you could have taken any class you wanted, what would it have been?

....

....

Grandchild

List all of the after-school clubs or sports that you participate in or have participated in:

....

....

....

If you could create your own after-school club, what would it be, and what would you do in it?

....

....

....

What school competitions or projects are you especially proud of, and why?

....

....

....

....

GRANDPARENT

List all of the after-school clubs or sports you participated in as a kid:

....

....

....

If you could've created your own after-school club when you were growing up, what would it have been, and what would you have done in it?

....

....

....

What school competitions or projects were you especially proud of, and why?

....

....

....

....

Q:

....

....

....

A:

....

....

....

....

....

....

....

Q:

A:

CHAPTER 6

Friends and Relationships

Grandchild

My best friend's name is ...., and we have been friends for .... years.

This is how we met:

....

....

....

What do you like most about your best friend?

....

....

....

What are some things you like to do together?

....

....

....

GRANDPARENT

My best friend's name is ...., and we have been friends for .... years.

This is how we met:

....

....

....

What do you like most about your best friend?

....

....

....

What are some things you like to do together?

....

....

....

Who are some of your other close friends?

....

....

....

What do you like to do with them?

....

....

....

What qualities are important to you in a friend?

....

....

....

....

GRANDPARENT

Who are some of your other close friends?

....

....

....

What do you like to do with them?

....

....

....

What qualities are important to you in a friend?

....

....

....

....

Grandchild

List all of the pets you have had, and an interesting fact about each one. If you haven't had a pet before, would you like one, and if so, what kind?

....

....

....

What are your favorite things to do with your pets? If you don't have pets, what can you imagine yourself doing with the pet you would like to have?

....

....

....

Tell a funny story about one of your pets or another pet you know:

....

....

....

....

GRANDPARENT

List all of the pets you have had, and an interesting fact about each one. If you haven't had a pet before, would you like one, and if so, what kind?

....

....

....

What are your favorite things to do with your pets? If you don't have pets, what can you imagine yourself doing with the pet you would like to have?

....

....

....

Tell a funny story about one of your pets or another pet you know:

....

....

....

....

Grandchild

Do you want to get married? If so, at what age? And if not, why not?

....

....

What qualities do you want your future husband or wife to have?

....

....

....

....

What do you think it will be like to be in love?

....

....

....

....

GRANDPARENT

Tell the story of how you met your spouse:

....

....

....

....

What are the qualities that attracted you to them?

....

....

....

How did you know you were in love with them?

....

....

....

Grandchild

Do you think you will want to have kids? If so, how many? If not, why not?

....

....

....

What do you think you will be like as a parent?

....

....

....

What qualities do you think parents should have?

....

....

....

....

GRANDPARENT

When you were little, did you think you would want to have children? If not, what made you change your mind?

....

....

....

....

Tell me a story about parenting my mom or dad when they were little:

....

....

....

....

....

Q:

A:

Q:

A:

CHAPTER 7
The Wider World

Grandchild

What are some major national and world events (such as presidential elections and historical firsts) that have happened in your lifetime?

....

....

....

....

....

Tell me a little bit more about a major event that affected you and how:

....

....

....

....

....

GRANDPARENT

What are some major national and world events (such as presidential elections and historical firsts) that have happened in your lifetime?

....

....

....

....

....

Tell me a little bit more about a major event that affected you and how:

....

....

....

....

....

Grandchild

Tell me about a service or charity project you've participated in. If you haven't done any volunteer work yet, how would you like to get involved in the future?

....

....

....

....

....

What political or social causes do you support? If you don't currently support any, which ones would you like to learn more about?

....

....

....

....

....

GRANDPARENT

Tell me about some of the service or charity projects you've participated in.

....

....

....

....

....

What are some of the major political or social causes that you have supported in your lifetime? How were you involved?

....

....

....

....

....

Grandchild

What inventions during your lifetime have changed your life? If you can't think of any recent ones, list some things you can't imagine living without.

....

....

....

....

....

What do you think needs to be invented, and how would it help improve our world?

....

....

....

....

....

GRANDPARENT

What were some big inventions during your lifetime? How did they change your life?

....

....

....

....

....

What do you think needs to be invented, and how would it help improve our world?

....

....

....

....

Grandchild

What famous people do you admire, and why?

....

....

....

....

What are some things that are popular now that you think you will find funny when you're older?

....

....

....

Tell me about a cultural trend or celebrity you're currently obsessed with:

....

....

....

GRANDPARENT

What famous people do you admire, and why?

....

....

....

....

What are some things that were popular when you were a kid that you now find funny?

....

....

....

Tell me about a cultural trend or celebrity you were obsessed with when you were my age:

....

....

....

Grandchild

If you could travel to any destination you have not yet visited, where would you go, and why?

....

....

....

....

Tell me a funny travel story—it can be about anything, from something you forgot to bring to something you saw for the first time.

....

....

....

....

....

GRANDPARENT

If you could travel to any destination you have not yet visited, where would you go, and why?

....

....

....

....

Tell me about your most memorable travel experience.

....

....

....

....

....

....

Q:

A:

Q:

A:

CHAPTER 8

Work and Career

Grandchild

What do you do to earn an allowance, and how much do you make? If you don't earn an allowance yet, what would you like to do to earn money?

....

....

Share any creative ways you have made money, like running a lemonade stand. If you haven't done something like this yet, what's one creative idea you have for making money?

....

....

Tell me a story about a big purchase you made with your allowance or earnings.

....

....

....

....

....

GRANDPARENT

If you earned money or an allowance as a child, share what you did and how much you earned.

....

....

What do you think earning money teaches children about finances?

....

....

Tell me a story about a big purchase you made with your allowance or earnings.

....

....

....

....

....

Grandchild

When I grow up, I want to be a ...., because ....

....

....

....

What do you think your parents want you to be?

....

....

What are some other careers you have considered?

....

....

....

....

GRANDPARENT

When you were a child, what did you want to be when you grew up, and why?

....

....

What do you think your parents wanted you to be?

....

....

How many jobs have you had, and what has your career path been like?

....

....

....

....

....

Grandchild

How old do you think you'll be when you get your first job, and what type of job do you think it will it be?

....

....

What do you think you will like about working?

....

....

....

What do you think you will *not* like about it?

....

....

....

GRANDPARENT

What do you (or did you) like about working?

....

....

....

What do you (or did you) *not* like about it?

....

....

....

Do you (or did you) ever wish you had picked a different career? If so, what and why?

....

....

....

Grandchild

What skills and personality traits do you already have that you think will help you be successful in your work life?

....

....

Which ones do you think you'll need to acquire or work on improving to be successful?

....

....

What do you think will be the hardest part of balancing a career with your other priorities, like hobbies, travel, or having a family?

....

....

....

....

....

GRANDPARENT

What skills and personality traits did you naturally have that helped you succeed in your career?

....

....

Which ones did you need to acquire or improve upon to be successful?

....

....

What was it like to balance a career with raising a family and other interests when you were younger?

....

....

....

....

Q:

A:

Q:

A:

CHAPTER 9

You and Me

Grandchild

My first memory of you is ....

....

....

....

....

My favorite memory of us together is ....

....

....

....

....

GRANDPARENT

My first memory of you is ....

....

....

....

....

My favorite memory of us together is ....

....

....

....

....

Grandchild

Here are a few of the things I like most about you:

....

....

....

....

....

This is my favorite activity we do together:

....

....

This is something I would like to do more with you:

....

....

GRANDPARENT

Here are a few of the things I like most about you:

....

....

....

....

....

This is my favorite activity we do together:

....

....

This is something I would like to do more with you:

....

....

Grandchild

We share these family traits:

....

....

....

Sometimes you remind me of .... and the way they

....

....

I see this special trait in you that I would like to develop more in myself:

....

....

....

....

GRANDPARENT

We share these family traits:

....

....

....

....

Sometimes you remind me of .... and the way they

....

....

I see this special trait in you that I would like to develop more in myself:

....

....

....

....

Grandchild

How would you describe me to someone who doesn't know me?

....

....

....

What do you like most about being my grandkid?

....

....

....

What do you think you will like most about being a grandparent someday?

....

....

....

GRANDPARENT

How would you describe me to someone who doesn't know me?

....

....

....

What do you like most about being my grandparent?

....

....

....

What did you like most about being a grandkid?

....

....

....

Grandchild

Over the course of completing this journal, I have learned these new things about you:

....

....

....

....

....

This is what our perfect day together would be like:

....

....

....

....

....

GRANDPARENT

Over the course of completing this journal, I have learned these new things about you:

....

....

....

....

....

This is what our perfect day together would be like:

....

....

....

....

Q:

....

....

....

A:

....

....

....

....

....

....

....

Q:

A:

CHAPTER 10

Hopes for the Future

Grandchild

In the future, I hope I do this (don't limit yourself; it can be anything!):

....

....

....

I hope I see this:

....

....

....

I hope to affect my community in this way:

....

....

....

122

GRANDPARENT

In the future, I hope you will do this:

....

....

....

I hope you will see this:

....

....

....

I hope you will affect your community in this way:

....

....

....

....

Grandchild

What changes do you see happening in the world in 10 years?

....

....

....

What are your hopes for the future of our planet?

....

....

....

Where do you look for inspiration about the future or in life?

....

....

....

GRANDPARENT

What changes do you see happening in the world in 10 years?

....

....

....

What are your hopes for the future of our planet?

....

....

....

Where do you look for inspiration about the future or in life?

....

....

....

Grandchild

These are three things I would like to get advice from you about:

1.

....

....

....

2.

....

....

....

3.

....

....

....

GRANDPARENT

These are my responses to the three things you wanted advice on:

1.

....

....

....

2.

....

....

....

3.

....

....

....

Q:

A:

Q:

A:

ABOUT THE AUTHOR

Scarlet Paolicchi lives in Nashville, Tennessee, where she enjoys the perfect combination of city life and access to the great outdoors. After a career in retail management, she founded Family Focus Blog, where for nearly a decade she has shared all things family related, from parenting advice and family dinner recipes to eco-living and family travel tips. She is wife to her Tulane University college sweetheart and mother to their two wonderful children. You can connect with her on Twitter and Instagram @familyfocusblog, or read more of her writing at familyfocusblog.com.

ABOUT THE ILLUSTRATOR

Irena Freitas is an illustrator from Manaus, Brazil. She loves illustrating the people and funny situations that she comes across in her daily life. She has an MFA in illustration from SCAD, and her clients include *Corriere della Sera, The New York Times, The Washington Post, BBC Brasil,* and *Folha de São Paulo.* Her illustrations have been selected by the Society of Illustrators and American Illustration.